WITHDRAWN
FROM THE RECORDS OF THE
MID-CONTINENT PUBLIC LIBRARY

draw cRaZy CrEaTuRes

kids DIY

steve barr

IMPACT
CINCINNATI, OHIO
www.impact-books.com

D1224119

Contents

MID-CONTINENT PUBLIC LIBRARY - QU

3 0003 13243565 0

Mid-Continent Public Library
15616 East US Highway 24
Independence, MO 64050

What You Need

- drawing paper
- pencils
- black felt-tip marker or pen
- crayons, colored pencils or colored markers
- pencil sharpener
- good eraser

How To Use This Book

This book will show you how to use basic lines and shapes to create cool crazy creatures. Feel free to change things around, experiment with different lines or shapes and make your drawings uniquely your own. The main thing to remember is to just have fun!

1 The first step in each lesson will appear in light blue.

2 The next step will be shown in red.

3 Blue and red pens were used to make the instructions easy to follow, but you should use a regular black pencil to create your creatures. Sketch lightly so you can easily erase extra lines later.

4 After you have finished drawing your crazy creature, erase any of the lines you do not need.

5 Use a black pen, black marker or a dark pencil to make bold outlines on your final sketch.

6 Adding color is the last step. Feel free to color your creation any way you wish. You do not have to mimic what I have done. I used pencils and markers to color my creatures, but you can use whatever materials you are comfortable with or happen to have around the house.

Basic Lines and Shapes

These are the basic lines and shapes you will use the most often as you create the creatures in this book. Practice them using different drawing tools, so you will get familiar with the different effects you can create with them. Don't worry if your lines and shapes don't turn out exactly like you want them to. The more you practice, the better you will become.

Feel free to switch things around a little bit when you're doing these lessons. If I drew a zigzag line but you'd rather use curved lines, that's okay! Experimenting with different looks will help you develop your creativity.

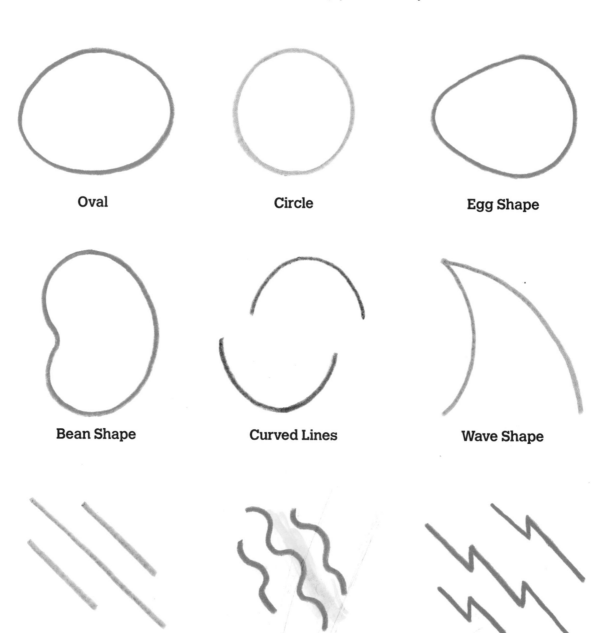

Oval	**Circle**	**Egg Shape**
Bean Shape	**Curved Lines**	**Wave Shape**
Straight Lines	**Squiggly Lines**	**Zigzag Lines**

Color

Mark Areas You Want to Color

Sometimes, if you're using crayons or colored pencils it can be a little difficult to add dark colors on top of light ones. To make it easier, mark out the areas you'd like to color first. You can leave white spaces on some of the sides to make it look like light is hitting your character.

Color the Dark Areas First

Color in the darkest areas first. You can even add color around your character's eyeballs to give him more personality.

Color Light Areas Next

Begin to fill in the lighter colors. If your color looks a little splotchy, just continue going back and forth across those areas until they appear smooth and even. Try going over it in a different direction than your first strokes—it will begin to fill in the white spaces.

Add Your Own Details to Finish

Once you get your cartoon completely colored, you're finished. If you want to, you can add a background or other details of your very own.

Inking

Start With a Thin Line

There are many different kinds of pens that artists can use to ink their drawings. When you're just starting out, any type of pen you want to use is fine. For the drawings in this book, I used a Flair felt-tip marker to outline the sketches first. This created a thin line.

Get Thicker

To get a bold line, I traced around the outside of my thin lines. With a little practice, you should be able to get very good at doing this.

Add Color

After I finished inking, I began to add color by lightly filling in the large areas.

Add Shade and Shadow

The final step is to add darker color for shading and a little bit of green under the monster's feet for a shadow.

Keep practicing your inking skills. As you get better, experiment with different pens and the lines they produce.

Experiment!

Experiment With Different Lines and Shapes

It's fine if you want to copy the creatures in this book exactly as I have drawn them. But you can also experiment with different lines and shapes to change them a little bit. For example, I used wave shapes on this creature, but perhaps you could try using curved lines instead.

Change Your Creature's Appearance

Using curved lines instead of wave shapes completely changes the creature's appearance.

Before

My original drawing was a hairy Big Foot kind of creature.

After

By changing the lines, I turned it into a swamp creature! You can also use colors to make your creations look very different from each other.

silly monster

Combine all sorts of lines and shapes to create a silly monster. You can follow this lesson exactly, or change some of the details to make your character different.

1 Draw a large semi-circle for the monster's body. Sketch ovals with small circles inside them to create the eyes.

2 Add curved lines on both sides of the head for horns. Use curved lines to add a mouth, jaw and tail.

3 Add curved lines inside the horns. Draw straight lines to begin the arms. Use curved lines for the legs and feet.

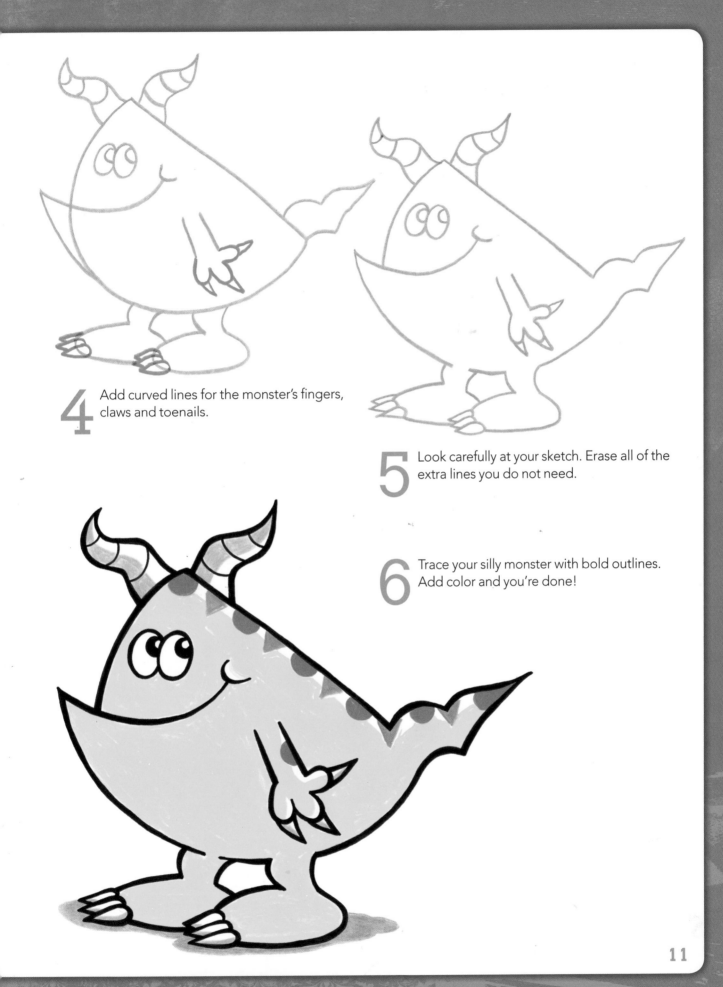

4 Add curved lines for the monster's fingers, claws and toenails.

5 Look carefully at your sketch. Erase all of the extra lines you do not need.

6 Trace your silly monster with bold outlines. Add color and you're done!

awesome alien

Some people claim they've had encounters with aliens. I have never seen one, so I'll just have to guess what one looks like. Let's draw an awesome alien!

1 Draw an oval for your alien's head. Use a semi-circle for its body.

2 Sketch curved lines on each side of the head. Add curved lines for a neck and legs.

3 Use straight lines for the arm, and a circle for the hand. Draw curved lines to create feet.

4 Sketch an oval with a circle inside it for the eye. Use straight lines for the fingers. Draw small circles on the end of each finger.

5 Erase all of the overlapping lines you do not need.

6 Trace your sketch with a bold outline. Add color, and your alien is complete!

flying pterodactyl

Imagine how crazy it would be to have lived in the age of dinosaurs—especially if a winged one was chasing you! Want to draw one? Here's how…

1 Draw an oval for the head and a semi-circle for the body.

2 Add curved lines to the front and back of the head. Use curved lines to create the neck, tail and legs.

3 Draw an oval with a circle inside for an eye. Sketch curved lines to add wings, feet and the tip of the tail.

4 Use curved lines for the toes and to add details to the front wing.

5 Erase any lines you don't need.

6 Draw a bold outline. Add color, and you've created a crazy flying dinosaur!

smiley shark

Cartoon creatures can act like humans. Sharks can even stand up and smile like people do. Let's draw a smiley shark.

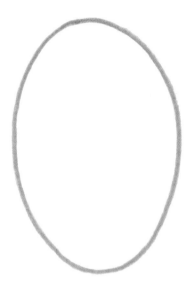

1 Draw an oval for the shark's body.

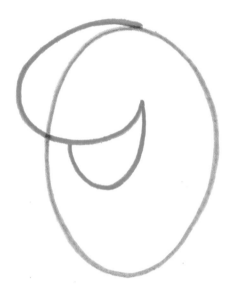

2 Add a big curved line for his snout, and a smaller curved line under that for his mouth.

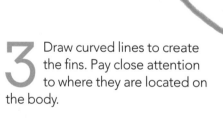

3 Draw curved lines to create the fins. Pay close attention to where they are located on the body.

4 Draw circles with dots inside for eyes. Add curved lines above the eyes for eyebrows. Then sketch straight lines inside the mouth to make teeth.

5 Erase any extra lines so that you are left with just the outlines needed for your shark.

6 Trace over your outline with bold lines and add color. You've created a really silly cartoon shark!

It's Okay to Add Human Features

Sharks don't actually have eyebrows, but that's okay. When creating crazy creatures, you can add human characteristics to animals to give them more personality.

lonely lizard

Even lizards get lonely sometimes. Let's create a cartoon lizard who looks a bit dejected. If you think she looks too sad, you can always curve her mouth upward in a smile.

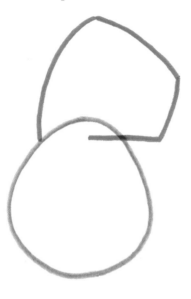

1 Draw a large oval for your lizard's body. Add curved lines above it to create the head.

2 Draw ovals with dots or small circles inside them for eyes. Sketch curved lines to add an arm, legs and a tail.

3 Draw curved lines on the head and the back. Add a wave shape on the tail for a spike.

4 Use curved lines for the toenails. Draw a curved line on the body and add straight lines to give her a segmented chest.

5 Erase all of the extra overlapping lines.

6 Add a bold outline, then color your lonely lizard. Perhaps you could draw a second lizard to hang out with her so she won't be so lonely.

happy piranha

Piranha are crazy fish with really sharp teeth. But, I think they're happy being piranha, so let's draw one with a big grin.

1 Sketch an egg shape with one side sort of tapered, like this example.

2 Draw curved lines to create the tail. Then use wave shapes to give him fins.

3 Sketch circles with little dots inside for eyes. Add curved lines above them for the eyebrows.

4 Draw curved lines to give him a wacky smile and a jaw that juts out. Use wave shapes to add sharp teeth.

5 Erase all of the extra lines. Look closely at the bottom fins. Get rid of the line going through the bottom left fin, but leave the line on the bottom right fin to make it look like it is on the other side of his body.

6 Put a nice bold stroke on your Piranha's outline, then add whatever colors you like. You can even draw several more fish to keep him company.

one-eyed monster

Crazy creatures don't have to look like regular animals. You can change all sorts of features on them to make them unique. Let's draw a monster with just one eye!

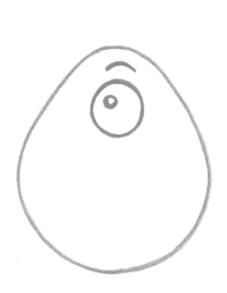

1 Draw a big egg shape for the monster's body. Draw a circle for an eye. Add an eyeball using a small circle inside another circle, then add a curved line for the eyebrow.

2 Sketch long curved lines on each side of the head for horns. Use straight lines for the arms and curved lines for the feet.

3 Draw wave shapes for the hair and teeth. Add curved lines on the ends of his arms for fingers and curved lines on his feet for toes.

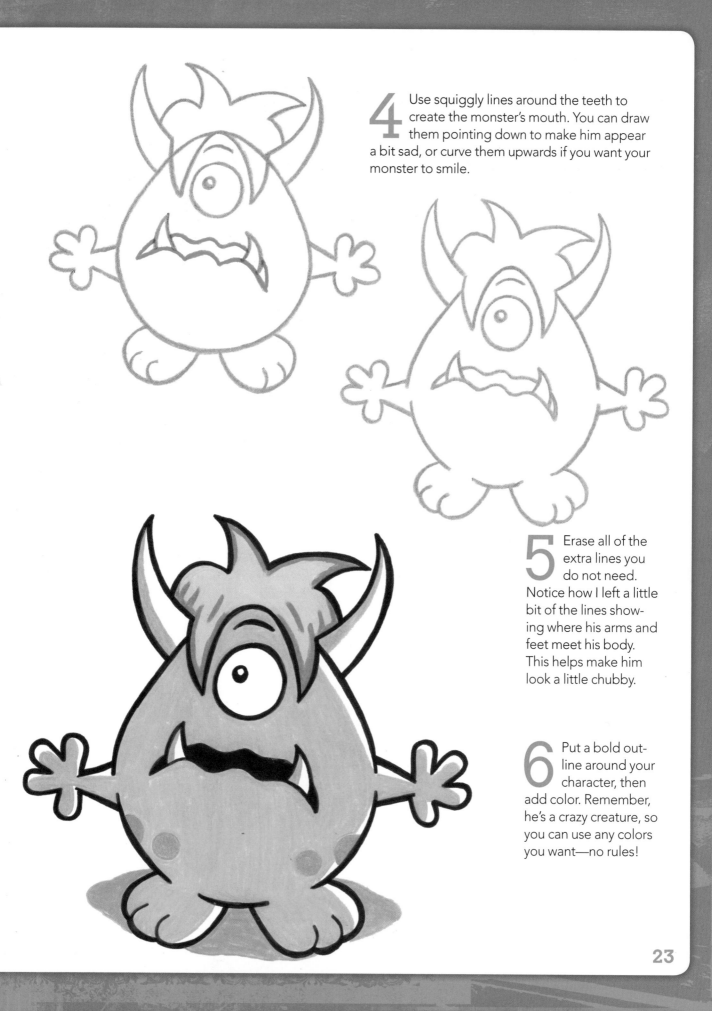

4 Use squiggly lines around the teeth to create the monster's mouth. You can draw them pointing down to make him appear a bit sad, or curve them upwards if you want your monster to smile.

5 Erase all of the extra lines you do not need. Notice how I left a little bit of the lines showing where his arms and feet meet his body. This helps make him look a little chubby.

6 Put a bold outline around your character, then add color. Remember, he's a crazy creature, so you can use any colors you want—no rules!

scared alien

Imagine that aliens visited Earth. I bet things would seem so unusual to them that some of them would get scared. Let's draw a frightened little visitor from another planet.

1 Draw a large circle for the body. Make two circles a bit above the body and add smaller circles inside them to make the eyes. Connect the eyes to the body using curved lines.

2 Sketch curved lines above the eyes for eyebrows. (He's so startled, his eyebrows have jumped off of his head!) Add straight lines for the arms and curved lines for the feet.

3 Use curved lines to give him fingers and toes. Put a big oval in the center of his body to create a wide open mouth.

4 Draw a curved line inside the top of his mouth for teeth. Use curved lines in the bottom of his mouth to make his tongue.

5 Erase all of the extra lines you do not need. Leave a little bit of the curved lines where his arms and feet meet his body.

6 Add a bold outline and color. Sketch teardrop shapes on each side of his head to make him look even more anxious. Add curved lines next to his hands to make it look like he's having a panic attack.

shy monster

Even monsters can be a little shy sometimes. In this lesson, we'll draw one.

1 Draw a large oval for the body. Use wave shapes to create ears. Look closely at how they're angled downward. Sketch curved lines on the bottom of the body for feet.

2 Sketch curved lines to give him big horns. Use curved lines on top of his head and along his side to make him hairy. Then add ovals with circles inside them for eyes, and curved lines for a tail.

3 Draw squiggly lines below his eyes for a mouth. Create arms using curved lines. Put curved lines on his feet for long, sharp toenails.

4 Add curved lines inside your monster's horns. Draw straight lines angled down towards the sides of his eyes. Then use straight lines joining in points to give him sharp claws.

5 Erase all of the extra lines. Leave a bit of the curved line between his feet to give him a little tummy.

6 Add a bold outline and color him in. Add color around his eyeballs to make him a little more endearing. He's pretty cute—for a monster!

mohawk monster

Monsters like to get wild and crazy with their hairdos sometimes. Let's try our hand at creating a monster with a Mohawk!

1 Start with a semi-circle with a straight line on the bottom for the head. Use an egg shape for your monster's body, then connect the head and body with curved lines for a neck.

2 Draw ovals for eyes. Put tiny dots inside them for eyeballs. Add curved lines at the bottom of the body for legs.

3 Use long curved lines above the head for his Mohawk. Draw curved lines above the eyes for eyebrows. Then add another curved line for his mouth and curved lines for an arm and the tail.

4 Make his Mohawk look a little hairier by adding curved lines inside it. Use curved lines to create sharp fingernails. Give him toenails by putting upside-down *U* shapes on his feet.

5 Erase all of the extra lines. Leave a little bit of the curved lines where his tail and legs meet his body.

6 Add a bold outline to your drawing, then color it. Use any color you want to. What a fine Mohawk he has!

sad monster

Monsters can get sad sometimes. Let's draw a sad little monster with a really big pout on her face.

1 Start by drawing a bean shape for the body. Use circles with small dots inside of them for eyes. If you make one eye slightly larger than the other, that will give her an even sillier look.

2 Use wave shapes on top of her head and on her back for hair. Draw curved lines for a tail, and use small bean shapes for the feet.

3 Sketch long curved lines on each side of her head to form horns. Draw an arm and fingers using curved lines. Add circles to the feet for toes.

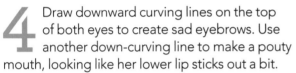 Draw downward curving lines on the top of both eyes to create sad eyebrows. Use another down-curving line to make a pouty mouth, looking like her lower lip sticks out a bit.

5 Get rid of all of the extra lines you do not need. Erase the left side of her second foot so that it looks like it's behind her stomach.

6 Add a dark outline around your monster, then color her.
   She looks like she needs a hug, but I'm not sure how monsters feel about hugging!

multi-eyed creature

Earlier, we drew a creature with only one eye. Now let's try drawing a creature with lots of eyes. While we're at it, let's give her a bunch of arms and legs too.

1 Draw a large bean shape for the body. Add three circles above the body for eyes. Attach them to the body with curved lines. (You can draw more eyes if you want to. After all, it's your drawing!)

2 Draw curved lines on the sides of each eye. Use circles inside the body to give your creature even more eyes. Add a curved line in the middle of the body for a smiling mouth.

3 Sketch semi-circles inside each eye for eyeballs. Add straight lines on both sides of the body for arms, as well as curved lines at the bottom of the body for legs.

4 Draw curved lines on the ends of the arms to give her hands and fingers. Use curved lines to create funky feet.

5 Erase the extra lines. Have the arms on your right extending slightly into the body to make them appear like they're on the front. But leave the lines on the other side to give it the appearance that those arms are behind her body.

6 Add a bold outline, then color your wacky creation. I bet nothing ever gets past this gal. She can keep an eye on everything going on all around her!

toad creature

Let's create a creature that looks like a toad. I always liked toads, but I don't think I'd ever want a gigantic one strolling towards me.

1 Draw a large oval for the body. Attach curved lines to the body to form his head.

2 Use circles for eyes. Make one slightly larger than the other. Put smaller circles inside the eyes for eyeballs.

3 Add curved lines on top of his head for tufts of hair. Draw a long curving line to create his mouth and give him a lip that is jutting out. Use curved lines for the legs.

4 Add small circles and dots to his body to give him warts. Draw curved lines at the bottom of his legs for feet.

5 Erase any extra lines you do not need. Erase small parts of the circles that form the warts.

6 Draw a bold outline, then add color. A tan color was used here because he's a toad-like creature, but you can use any colors you like. You can also put a little shadow under each of the warts to make them look raised.

He seems kind of friendly with that big smile on his face, but I'd hate to see him when he's "hopping" mad!

growling goblin

Some creatures act scary just to intimidate people. They wave their arms around and make scary noises. It's best to just ignore them, but I doubt that I could ignore this guy.

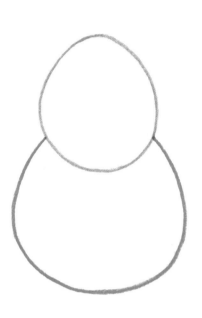

1 Draw an egg shape for the head. Add a large egg shape or oval below it for the body.

2 Use long curved lines on each side of the head for ears. Sketch small circles with dots inside them for eyes. Create arms and legs using curved lines.

3 Sketch curved lines above the head for eyebrows. Draw a peanut shape below his eyes for a mouth. Add curved lines to the arms for hands and thumbs. Use ovals on the bottom of the legs for feet.

4 Use curved lines inside of his mouth for teeth. Draw curved lines inside the body to begin his clothes, then add zigzag lines to the bottom to complete his outfit. Sketch semi-circles on his feet for toes.

5 Erase extra overlapping lines, but leave some of the lines where his arms meet his body.

6 Draw a bold outline around your goblin. Then add any colors you wish. That guy sure has some serious gaps between his teeth—I hope he sees a dentist soon!

dancing dinosaur

Let's draw a really happy dancing dinosaur.

1 Draw an oval for the head. Use a semi-circle for his belly and a straight line for his back.

2 Sketch curved lines to create his nose, eyes and bony forehead. Add curved lines for arms and legs. (Note the position of his legs and duplicate that.)

3 Put a curved line below his nose to give him a big smile. Draw curved lines on his arms for hands, and use curved lines for his tail.

4 Use curved lines on your dinosaur's head, back and tail to give him spikes. Sketch small *U* shapes for toenails. Add a curved line on the leg inside his body so it looks like you're seeing the bottom of his foot.

5 Erase all of the lines you do not need.

6 Add a bold outline and color. Use small curved lines beside his hands and long curved lines on either side of his body to make it look like he's moving back and forth.

It would probably be really entertaining to watch a dinosaur dance. But maybe it would be better to head for the hills, because there's a good chance it would cause an earthquake!

angry dragon

Whatever you do, never get a dragon mad. Let's draw an angry dragon so you'll know what one looks like if you ever cross paths.

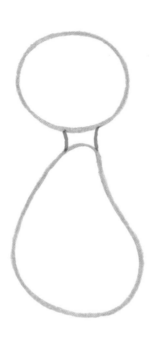

1 Draw a circle for your dragon's face. Sketch an oval for the body, but curve one side of it in a little bit. Connect the head and body using curved lines for a neck.

2 Put curved lines on his head to give him lumps above his eyes and create his big nose. Add a circle with a dot inside it for an eye. Use curved lines to create his legs, feet and tail.

3 Sketch long curved lines on his head for horns. Use ovals for nostrils. Add a downward curving line on the top of his eye. Draw straight lines for arms. Use curved lines on his chest and then upside-down *U* shapes for toenails.

4 Use straight lines to create his gritted teeth. Add straight lines to his back for spikes. Draw curved lines on the ends of his arms for hands.

5 Erase any lines you no longer need. Leave some lines where the front leg meets the body and tail.

6 Add a bold outline and color. You can make him a little scarier looking by making the whites of his eyes yellow. To make him look even angrier, use curved lines to make a little steam coming out of his nose.

Now that is one really, really grumpy dragon! It would probably be a good idea to move on to another page and draw a different creature.

stinky swamp creature

You never know what might come crawling out of the muck in a swamp. Let's just hope it's not one of the crazy creatures we're going to draw in this lesson!

1 Draw an oval overlapping a smaller circle to create the eyes. Add small circles inside them for eyeballs. Then use a big oval or egg shape for the body and connect it to the eyes using curved lines.

2 Put curved lines above the eyes for eyebrows. Add a big bean shape inside the body for an open mouth.

3 Use straight lines for sharp teeth. Put curved lines on the sides of his body for arms. Draw curved lines on each side of the body.

4 Sketch curved lines on the arms to make hands. Add curved lines to the body and arms to make them look like they're dripping with ooze. Draw some circles inside the body, then use curved lines inside the mouth for a tongue.

5 Erase any extra lines, including parts of the small circles on the body. This will make them stand out a bit more.

6 Draw a bold outline, then add color. Use wobbly lines above the hands to make your creature look stinky. Add curved lines near the bottom of the body to make it look like a shaking blob.

Whew! This creature looks like he could use a bath. Let's move on to the next lesson before he gets too close.

sprinting dinosaur

Even dinosaurs need to keep in shape and get a little exercise every now and then. We've drawn a dancing dinosaur—now let's draw one running.

1 Draw a circle to begin the dinosaur's head. Create her body using a semi-circle and a straight line. Connect the two using tilted straight lines for a neck.

2 Sketch an oval with two small semi-circles inside it for an eye. Put a curved line above it for a ridge. Use curved lines to create her nose, arms and legs. Look closely at how they are positioned.

3 Draw a curved line to complete her open mouth. Add curved lines to form hands on the ends of the arms. Use long curved lines to create the tail.

4 Draw straight lines that join in points on the back of her head, back and tail. Make toenails with curved lines on the bottom of her legs.

5 Erase all extra lines. Pay close attention to where the lines on the arms and body meet, so you can create the illusion that one arm is in the front and the other is on the opposite side of the body.

6 Add a bold outline and color. You can make it look like she's really moving if you draw a big drop of sweat flying behind her head. Add straight lines and curved lines to form a cloud of dust behind her.

If you put distance between her shadow and her legs, she'll look like she's moving so fast her feet aren't even touching the ground.

goofy gator

When you accidentally bump your head, sometimes it can make you feel a little goofy. Let's draw a funny alligator that just took a little bonk to his head.

1 Draw an oval for the base of your gator's head, and use curved lines to form the top of his head. Add more curved lines to create his body.

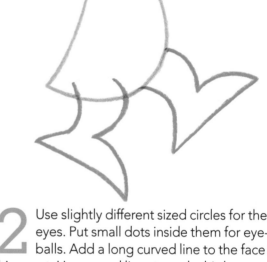

2 Use slightly different sized circles for the eyes. Put small dots inside them for eyeballs. Add a long curved line to the face for his snout. Use curved lines to make his legs and feet.

3 Draw curved lines to create a tongue, nostrils and teeth. Then add curved lines to his abdomen to give him a segmented chest.

4 Sketch straight lines for his arms. Add curved lines at the ends of the arms to make his fingers. Draw a curved line on his back for the tail.

5 Erase the extra lines. Pay close attention to make sure you leave his teeth in front of his arm.

6 Draw a bold outline, then add color. Make your gator look dizzy by putting curved lines and stars around his head. Adding little curved lines near his feet and arms will make him look even wobblier.

bashful bigfoot

People say that Bigfoot does not exist, but I know how to prove them wrong—let's draw him. Once we create him, he'll exist. Nobody can argue with that logic.

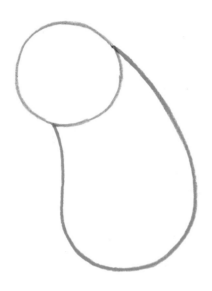

1 Draw a circle for the head. Add long curved lines to form the body.

2 Sketch a curved line for his nose. Use an oval with small semi-circles inside it for his eye. Then add a curved line for the top of his mouth and curved lines for his legs and feet.

3 Draw curved lines to complete his mouth and give him a jaw that juts out. Use more curved lines to add arms, hands and toes.

4 Draw wave shapes all along his head, back, arms and legs to make him really hairy. Add a wave shape above his eye. Used a curved line for his nostril and straight lines for his teeth.

5 Erase all extra lines. Remember to leave a few small lines where the arms and legs meet the body.

6 Add a bold outline to your drawing, then color it. Use any color you like.

See, Bigfoot exists. There he is!

friendly gremlin

From what I hear, gremlins can be very friendly unless you feed them. Let's draw a gremlin, but be very careful not to leave any snacks laying around.

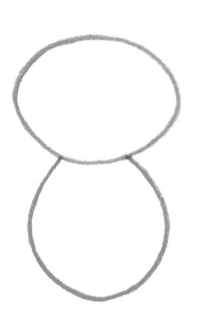

1 Draw an oval for your gremlin's head. Add another oval or egg shape below it to form the body.

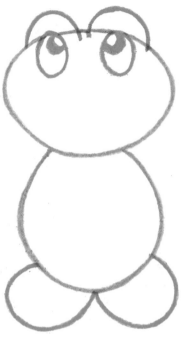

2 Use ovals for eyes. Draw small semicircles inside the eyes for eyeballs. Add curved lines above the eyes for eyebrows and curved lines below the body for feet.

3 Sketch long curved lines on each side of his head for ears. Use a small curved line just below the eyes for a nose. Add straight lines for arms.

4 Use two curved lines below his nose for a mouth. Add curved lines to the ends of each arm for fingers.

5 Draw wave shapes on top of his head to make his hair sticking up. Put curved lines on his feet for toes.

6 Erase all of the extra lines. Pay close attention to the lines where his arms and feet meet his body.

7 Instead of adding a bold outline this time, let's try something a little different. Use shaky lines like the ones that are shown in this example. This will let us make him look really hairy.

8 Now go around those shaky lines with a slightly bolder outline. You don't have to do it on his eyes, nose or mouth, just on the edges of his body.

9 Wow—he's a really hairy little gremlin! Add color, and you're done.

Crazy Coloring!

You've completed all of the drawing lessons in this book. Now have some fun practicing your coloring skills on the creatures on the following pages.

Certificate of Accomplishment

Has successfully completed the "Draw Crazy Creatures" course and is now fully qualified to be known as a "Crazy Cartoonist"!

Date: _____

Instructor: _Steve Barr_

Photograph by Dave Sykes

About the Author

Steve Barr is a professional cartoonist. People actually pay him to draw funny pictures! He lives in the mountains of North Carolina in a little cabin that is his office and his studio. Steve's cartoons have appeared in all sorts of publications, including a lot of newspapers and magazines. He's designed greeting cards and board games. His background also includes writing and drawing a nationally syndicated comic strip, doing key cells for animation and creating advertising art.

In his spare time, Steve likes to go out and search for cool rocks and minerals. When he's not doing that, you can find him at home doodling just for fun.

Dedication

Dedicated to Wendy Hall, my Muse.

Acknowledgments

I'd like to thank everyone at F+W Media who played a role in making this book possible. Special thanks go out to Christina Richards for her wonderful editing, Wendy Dunning for her great design work, Mark Griffin for his production coordination and Pam Wissman for helping make this all happen. I'd like to also tip my hat to Dave Sykes for snapping the photo of me that appears on this page.

Draw Crazy Creatures. Copyright © 2013 by Steve Barr. Manufactured in China. All rights reserved. No part of this book may be reproduced in any form or by any electronic or mechanical means including information storage and retrieval systems without permission in writing from the publisher, except by a reviewer who may quote brief passages in a review. Published by IMPACT Books, an imprint of F+W Media, Inc., 10151 Carver Road, Suite 200, Blue Ash, Ohio, 45242. (800) 289-0963. First Edition.

 Other fine IMPACT Books are available from your favorite bookstore, art supply store or online supplier. Visit our website fwmedia.com.

17 16 15 14 13   5 4 3 2 1

DISTRIBUTED IN CANADA BY FRASER DIRECT
100 Armstrong Avenue
Georgetown, ON, Canada L7G 5S4
Tel: (905) 877-4411

DISTRIBUTED IN THE U.K. AND EUROPE
BY F&W MEDIA INTERNATIONAL LTD
Brunel House, Forde Close, Newton Abbot,
TQ12 4PU, UK
Tel: (+44) 1626 323200, Fax: (+44) 1626 323319
Email: enquiries@fwmedia.com

DISTRIBUTED IN AUSTRALIA BY CAPRICORN LINK
P.O. Box 704, S. Windsor NSW, 2756 Australia
Tel: (02) 4560-1600
Fax: (02) 4577-5288
Email: books@capricornlink.com.au

Edited by Christina Richards
Designed by Wendy Dunning
Production coordinated by Mark Griffin

Metric Conversion Chart

To convert	to	multiply by
Inches	Centimeters	2.54
Centimeters	Inches	0.4
Feet	Centimeters	30.5
Centimeters	Feet	0.03
Yards	Meters	0.9
Meters	Yards	1.1

Ideas. Instruction. Inspiration.

Download a FREE bonus lesson at impact-books.com/drawcrazycreatures.

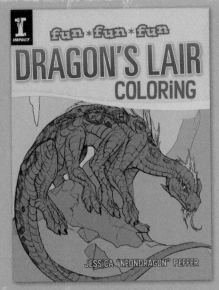

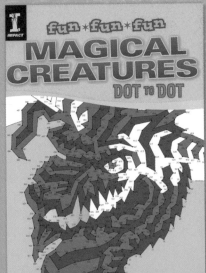

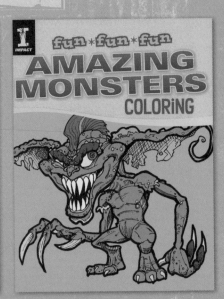

Check out these IMPACT titles at impact-books.com!

These and other fine **IMPACT** products are available at your local art & craft retailer, bookstore or online supplier. Visit our website at impact-books.com.

Follow **IMPACT** for the latest news, free wallpapers, free demos and chances to win FREE BOOKS!

IMPACT-BOOKS.COM

- ▸ Connect with your favorite artists
- ▸ Get the latest in comic, fantasy and sci-fi art instruction, tips and techniques
- ▸ Be the first to get special deals on the products you need to improve your art

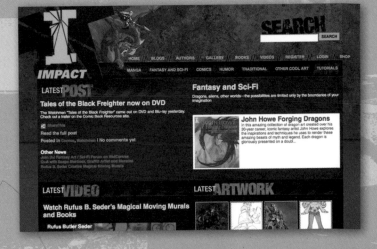